MW01435802

ALWAYS BE YOUR BEST YOU

Written by
Warren G. Landrum

Illustrated by
Amara Naybab

WARLAND BOOKS
Grand Prairie, Texas

ALWAYS BE YOUR BEST YOU
Published by:
Warland Books
Email: warrenglandrum@hotmail.com

Warren Landrum, Publisher Cover and Interior
Artistic Conceptualization: Carol Landrum
Yvonne Rose/Quality Press.info, Book Packager
Illustrator: Amara Naybab

All rights reserved No part of this book may be reproduced or transmitted in any form or by any means electronic or mechanical, including photocopying, recording or by any information storage and retrieval system without written permission from the author, except for the inclusion of brief quotations in a review.

Copyright ©2021 by Warren Landrum
Hardcover ISBN #: 978-1-0880-0935-2
Library of Congress Control Number: 2018913347

DEDICATION

This book is dedicated to those who are
already "being their best you"…
and to those about to!

INTRODUCTION

This book came about as the result of a little motivational phrase I came up with to continually encourage my granddaughter, Mia. I wanted her to always do the best she could in everything she did, so on August 11th, I grabbed a sheet of notebook paper, and as carefully, as I could, I wrote the words, "Mia, Be Your Best You" – Papa. My intent was to get a frame, which I did, and put the frame on her desk, where she would constantly be reminded of this sentiment.

A few weeks passed, and as I looked at the paper getting ready to actually make the final "frame-ready" draft, a thought came to me.

"Why not share this sentiment and message with EVERYONE?" So that's what I did!!

That original doc is shown on the following page:

MIA,
BE
YOUR
BEST
YOU!

8-11-2021

PAPA

"I'm tired of practice, Papa," Mia said,
as she sat at the piano one day.

"Practice Mia!"

"But if you don't practice, Mia, you'll never learn to play. Let me tell you what I'm talking about."

DANCERS DON'T NEED WINGS TO FLY.

"When you do your ballet lessons,
and plie across the floor,

If you don't practice in the mirror,
you'll fail at that, for sure!"

"But sometimes, I get tired.
I just want to go outside and play.

Why do I have to practice,
almost each and every day?"

"It's okay to play outside, Mia.
In fact it's healthy for you.

"Be your best."

But you've got to have a balance in everything you do. ALWAYS BE YOUR BEST YOU."

"You mean, like even with my Spelling, when my teacher taught us to spell?

And then I'd come home and work with Nana, to make sure I did that well?"

"Yes, that's what I'm talking about Mia.
Just try to make your practice fun.

Then the more and more you practice, the easier it will become. ALWAYS BE YOUR BEST YOU!"

Swimming Practice Pool

"But what about my swimming, Papa?
Do I have to practice that, too?

I already can do a Cannonball,
and swim up and down the pool!"

"Mia, practice will make you this fast."

"You know we just watched the Olympics, Mia and those girls swam very fast.

The practice that you do today, will make sure your Swimming Skills last. ALWAYS BE YOUR BEST YOU!"

"Mix Red & Blue to get Purple Mia."

"You know one thing that I love, Papa, is to make paintings and do my art.

I like to work with Nana, but sometimes we don't know where to start."

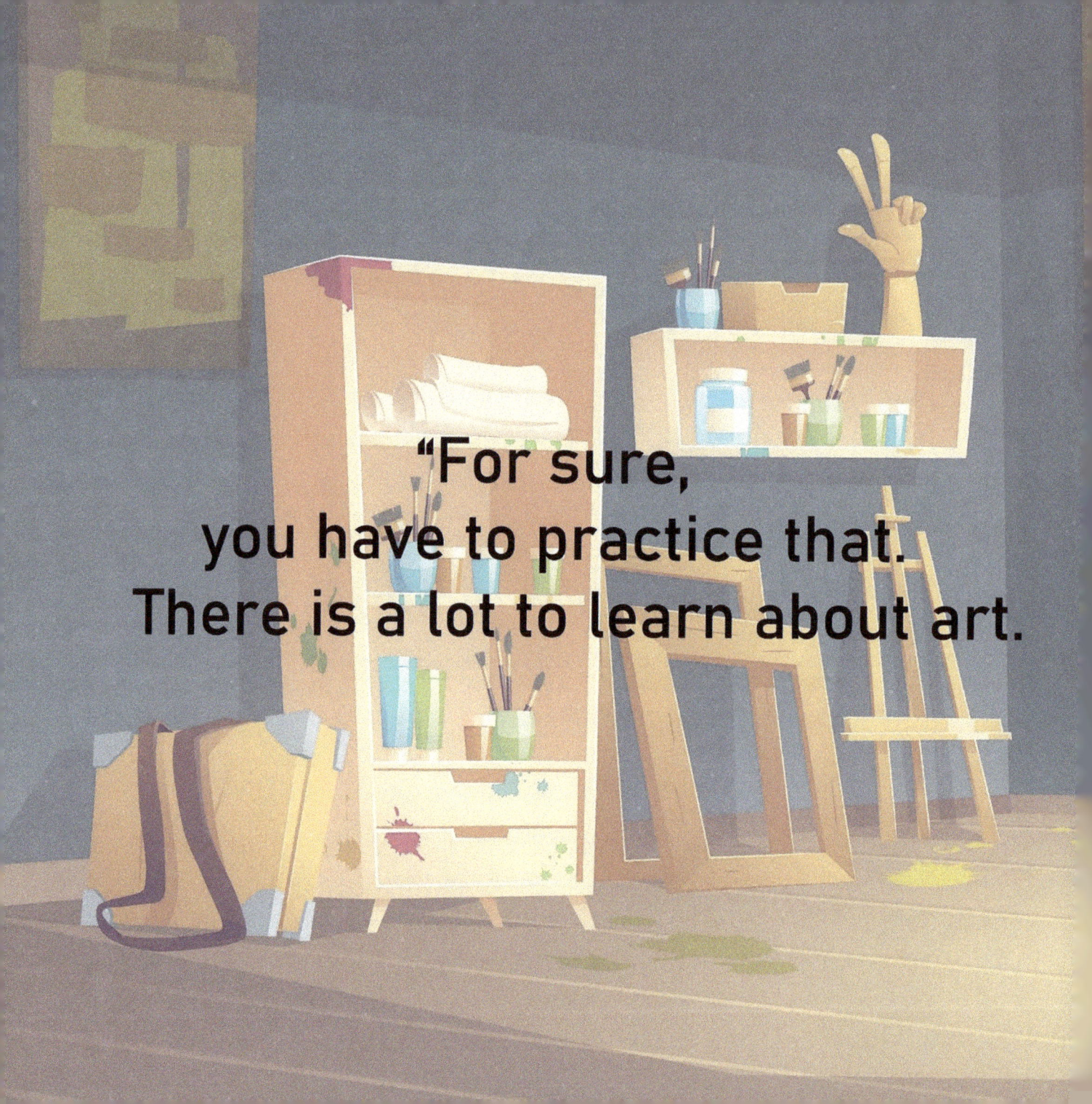

"For sure,
you have to practice that.
There is a lot to learn about art.

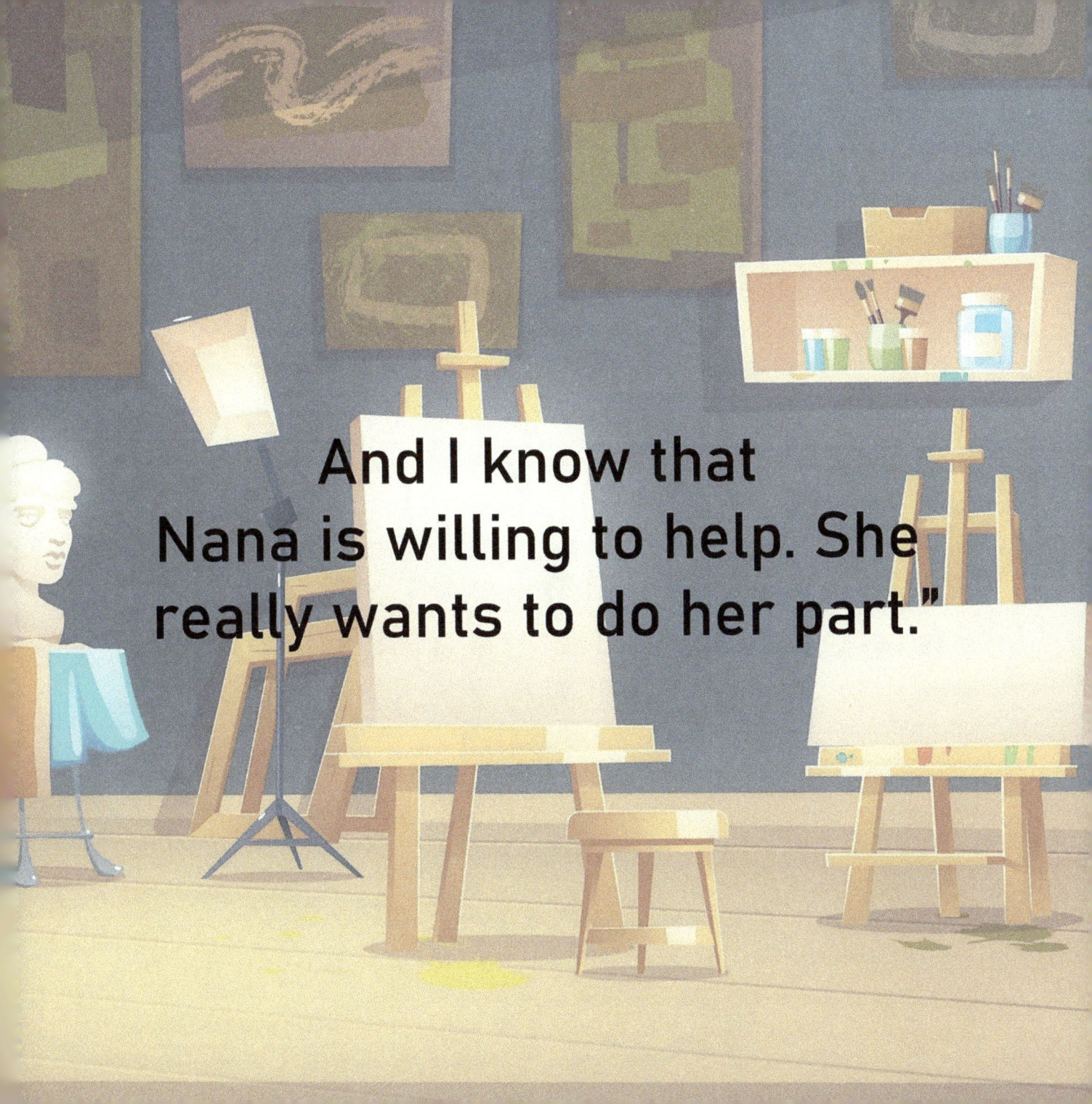

And I know that Nana is willing to help. She really wants to do her part."

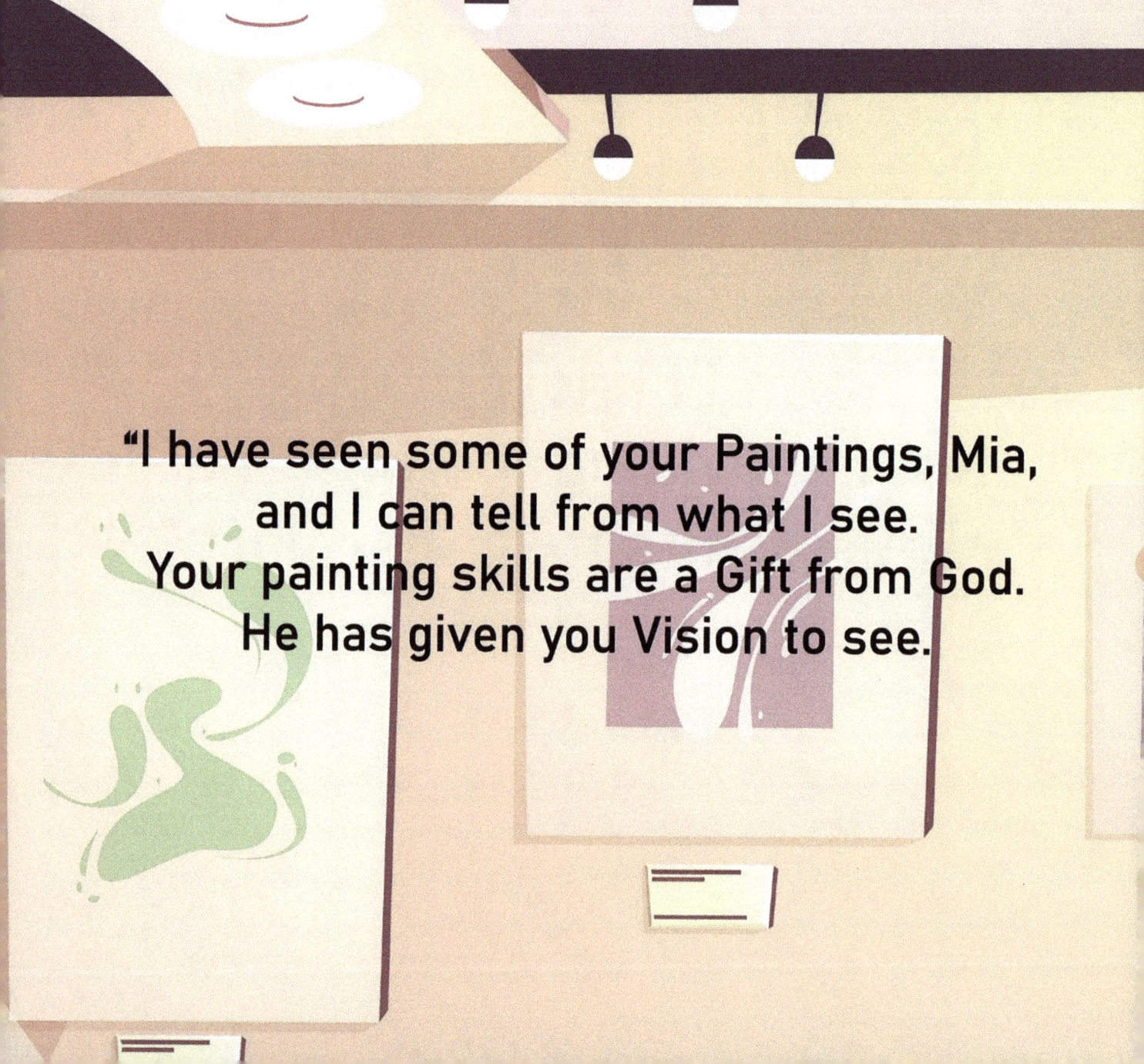

"I have seen some of your Paintings, Mia,
and I can tell from what I see.
Your painting skills are a Gift from God.
He has given you Vision to see.

You see Shapes and Colors and Lights.
You have a Gift, no doubt.
But you have to practice even that, to make sure your Flame doesn't die out.
ALWAYS BE YOUR BEST YOU!"

"Oh, I get it now Papa," Mia said.
"For anything I really want to do, I have to practice, practice, practice – to make you proud – And Nana and Mommy, too!

"That's my genius grand daughter!"

But I also want to do my best, 'cause it makes me feel good, too. And I really like being the best, you KNOW I don't like Number Two! I **WILL** ALWAYS BE MY BEST ME!!"

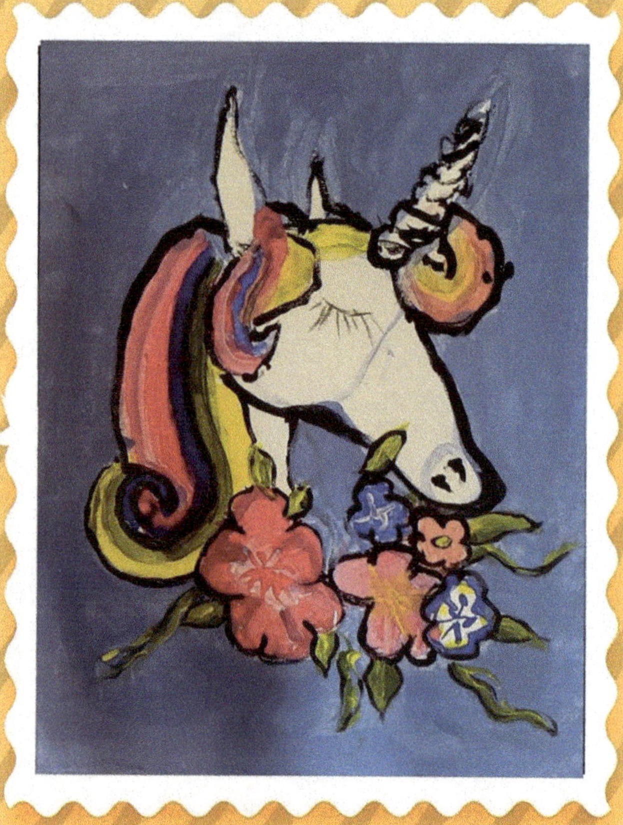
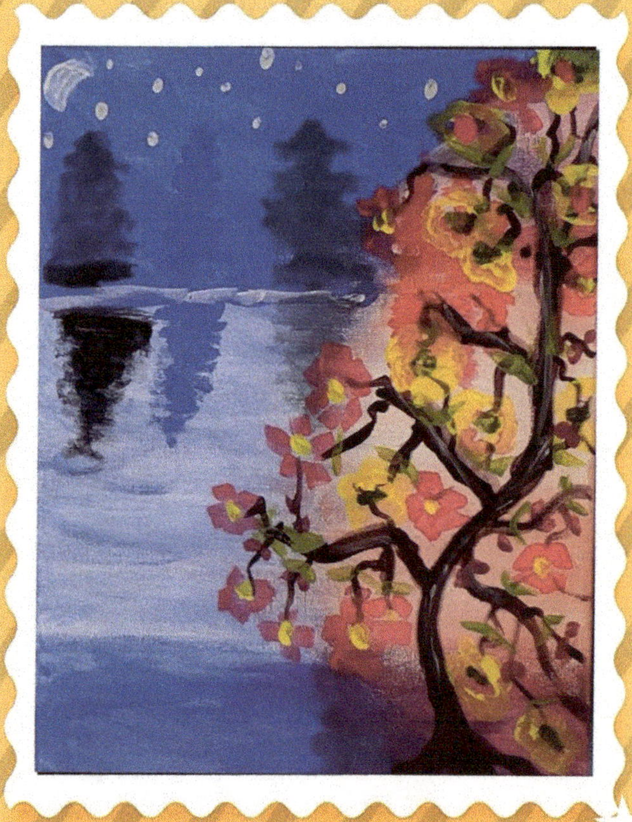

APPENDIX A

Some of Mia's artwork (ages 6 and 7)

Dana

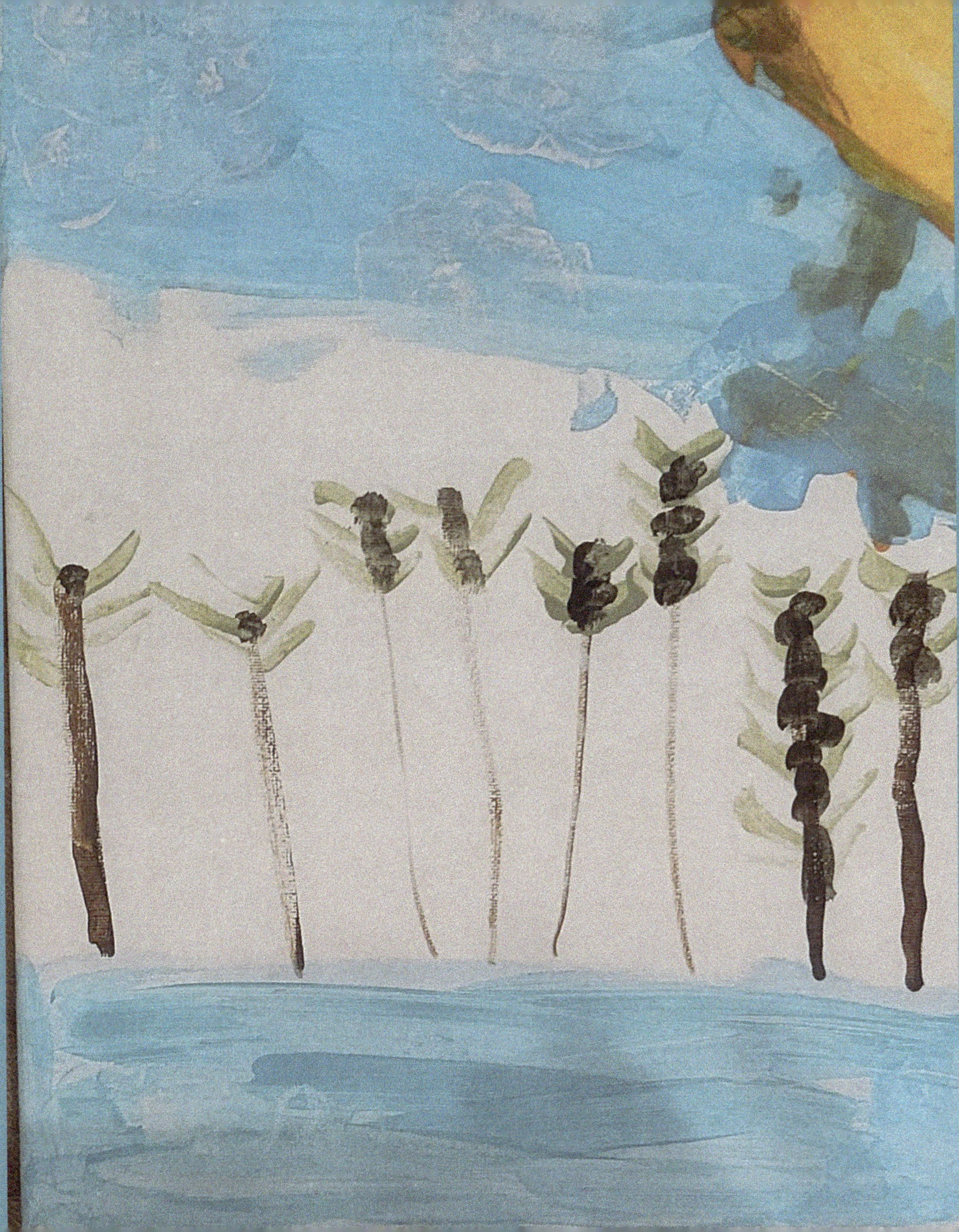

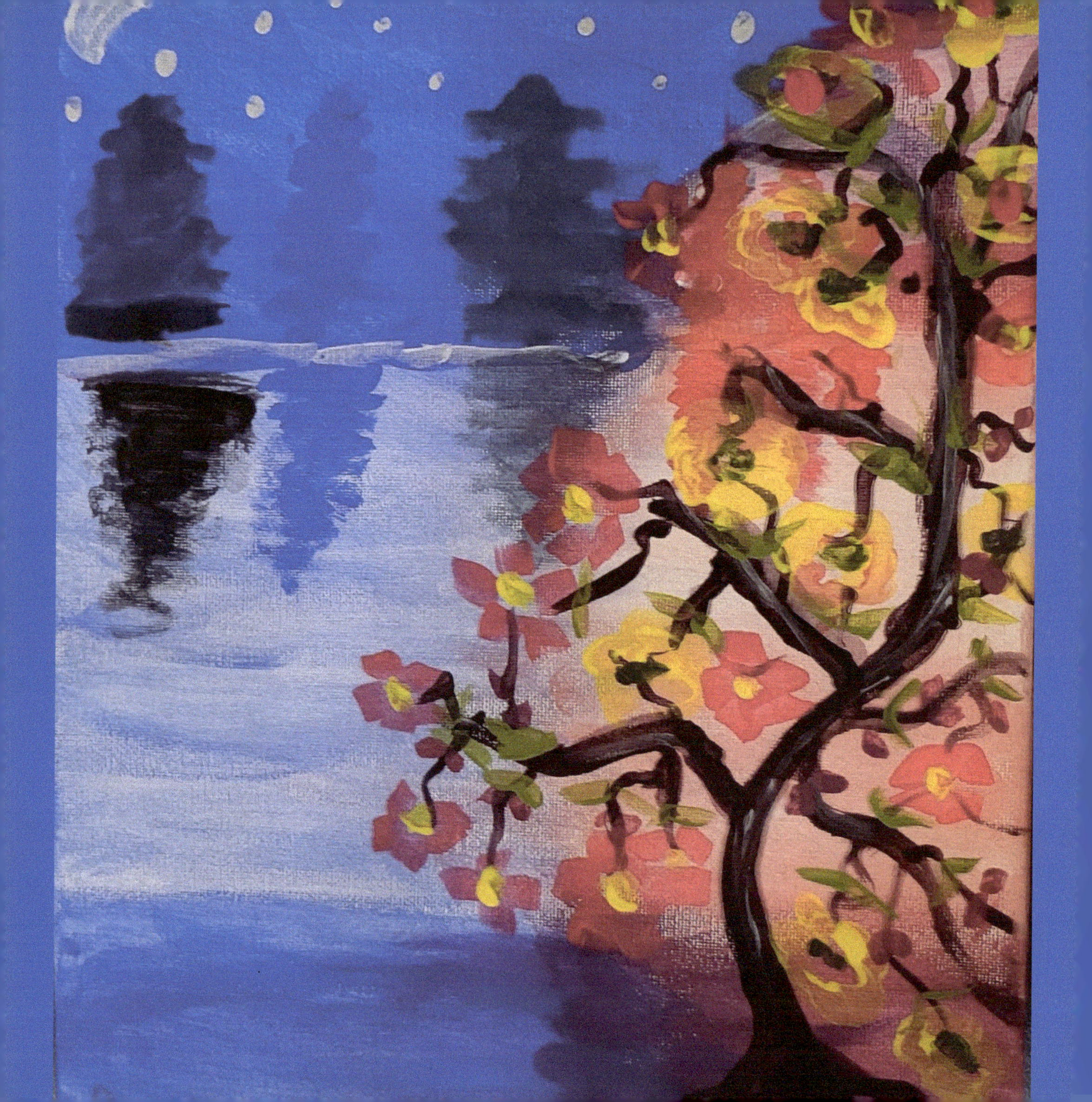

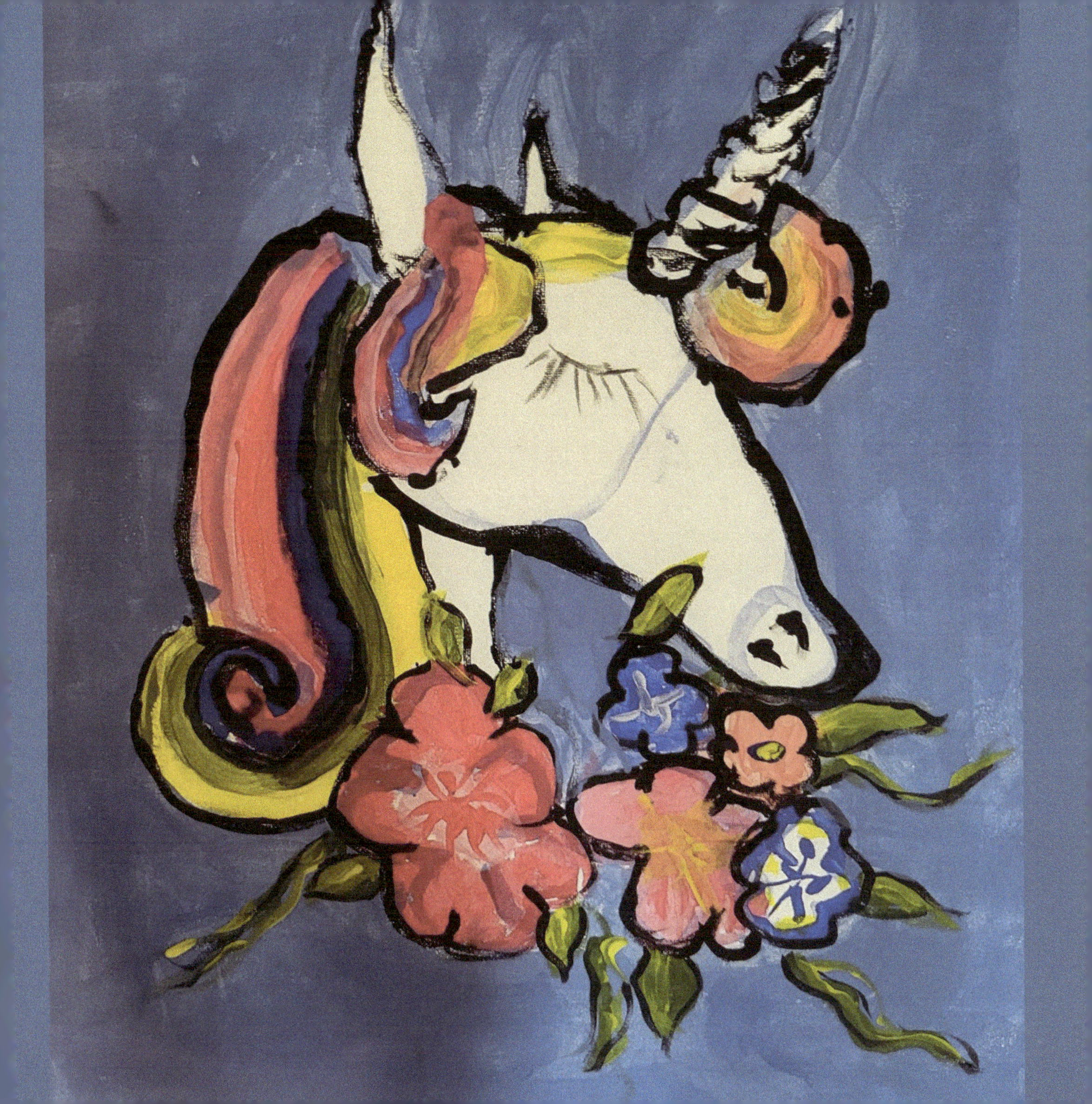

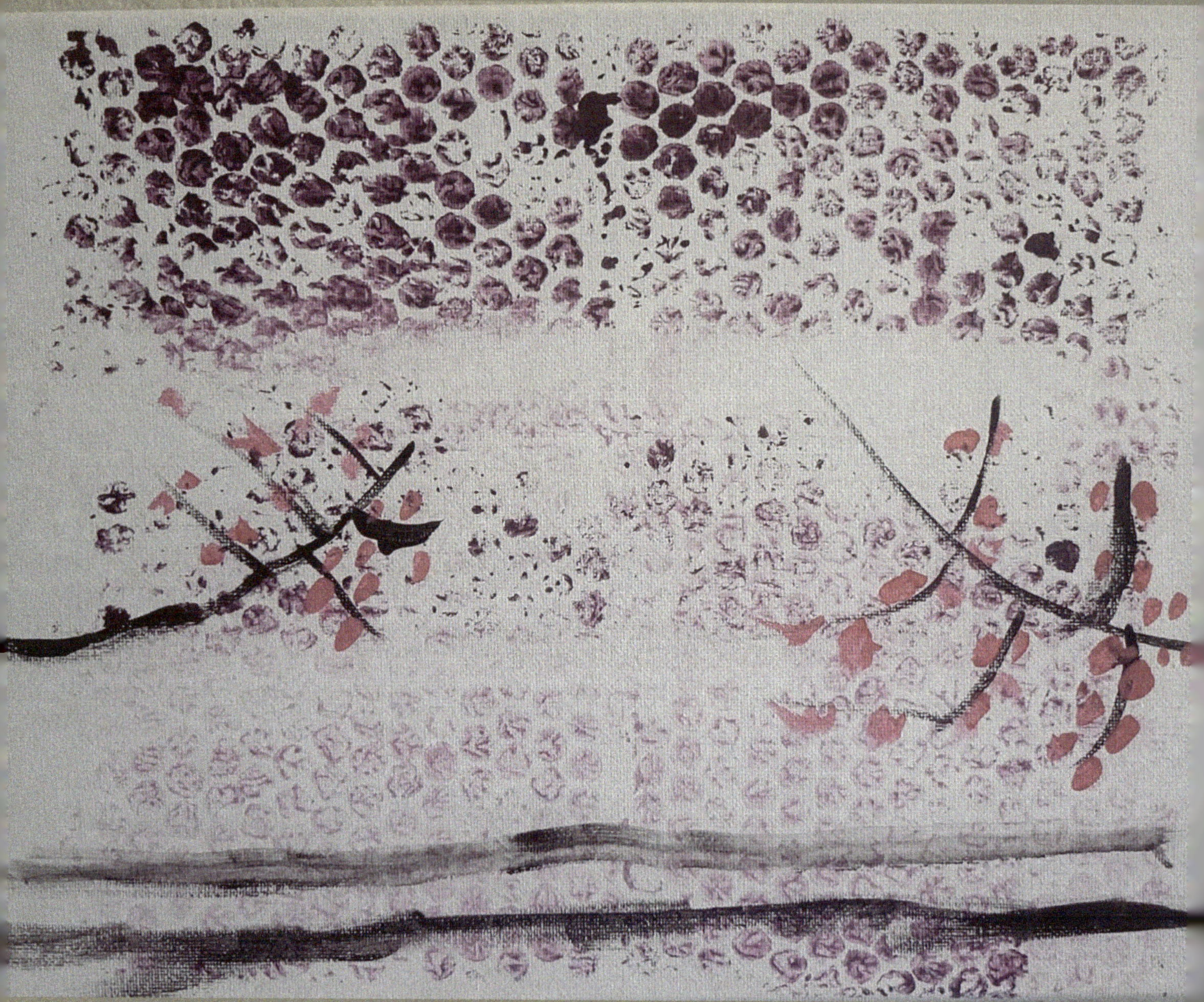

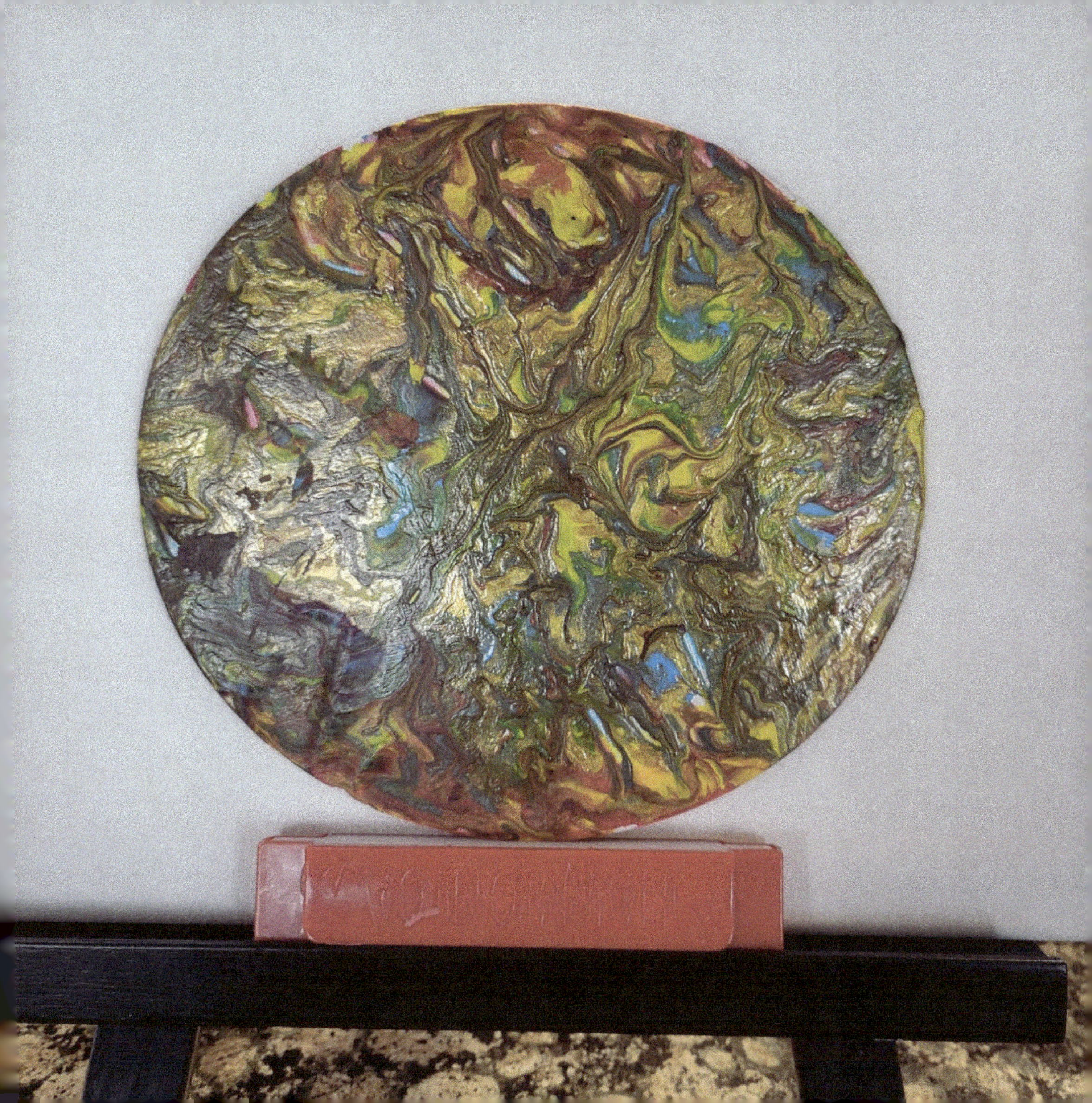

APPENDIX B

Mia practicing at the piano

APPENDIX C

Academic Excellence

```
                    Cora Spencer Elementary
                    3140 S. Camino Lagos
                    Grand Prairie, TX 75054
                    Phone:   817-299-6680
                    Principal : Jocelyn Hobdy


                                                    Danae M. Sheckleford
                                                          Grade: 02


                                                    1st Six Weeks 2021-22

Entity: 121      1ST
HOMEROOM 2ND-NR  E
  Rubio,J
LANGUAGE ARTS    98
  Rubio,J
MATH             100
  Rubio,J
SCIENCE          95
  Rubio,J
SOCIAL STUDIES   100
  Rubio,J
ART              100
  Ferguson,S
MUSIC            100
  Moore,J
PHYSICAL EDUCAT  100
  Preusser,J
```

ABOUT MIA SHECKLEFORD

Mia being her best in Cap and Gown graduating from pre-school a couple years ago

Our 7-year old Mia is the Apple of our Eyes. She was born Danae Mia Sheckleford on August 12, 2014, in Arlington, Texas to her parents, the late Dwight and Suzette (our daughter) Sheckleford, but she has been Mia to her grandfather "Papa" and me since the day she was born.

Mia is very outgoing, always smiling, and always wants to be a part of what's going on. For example, "Nana, can I help you with that? Can I mix the cake for you? Can I flip the fritter?" Sometimes I am scared, but allow her to do so under supervision and she does well.

She is very active at school. When I pick her up from school, she starts to open up her bag to show me her work for the day and week. She takes pleasure in showing me her math and phonics tests and telling me that she got 100%.

At 3-years old, Mia took private swimming lessons. The following summer we tried to take her back, but her response was, "No Nana. I can already swim." And sure enough, she has improved on her own since then, and is now swimming like a fish.

Mia tells me that she wants to be a Cardiac Nurse like me. I tell her that she can be anything she wants to be. She has a heart of gold, is always smiling, is very polite, and is loved by all – family, friends, and teachers. All because she is ALWAYS BEING THE BEST Mia!

… **Nana**

ABOUT THE AUTHOR

Warren G. Landrum, Jr. is an Award-Winning Author, Editor, Poet, Air Force vet, Community Activist, Alpha Phi Alpha fraternity member, Husband, Dad, and Grandfather. He was born and raised in the steel-mill town of East Chicago, Indiana and currently resides in Grand Prairie, Texas.

Warren's degrees include an Associate in Information Systems and Computer Programming from Purdue University and a Bachelor's in Management from the University of Phoenix. This educational foundation allowed him to flourish in his career in Information Technology, allowing him to travel all over the world setting up computer systems.

Warren is also the owner of CRUISE Control, an Independent Cruise Travel Agency.

Warren has written and published 9 books prior to this one:

"The Heart & Soul of a Black Man,"

"Let's Go Home to Indiana Harbor: Reflections From Mid-Town America,"

"Texas Politics – Grand Prairie Style: Campaign 2013",

"Stroke of Grace: The Juaquin Hawkins Story,"

"Mia Goes to Jamaica: An ABC Journey,"

"Nine Days in Italy: The Highs and Lows of Driving Through Italia" (3rd-Place Winner in Adult Non-Fiction category at 2018 North Texas Book Festival in Denton, TX) which he co-wrote with his wife Carol, "Nine Days in Paris: The Journey Continues" (2nd-Place Winner in Adult Non-Fiction category at 2019 North Texas Book Festival in Denton, TX) and "Nine Days in Singapore: A Family Affair." The last 3 are a part of his Travel Series.

"A Corona Love Affair," is Warren's first novel - released in August of 2020.

Warren believes that his Purpose in Life is simply to make people smile – whether by taking them along with him to some tropical paradise through his books, or actually sending them there through his cruise company, or simply giving them a Kind Word or a Warm Smile.

Warren's hobbies and passions are Reading, Writing, and Traveling, which he can't wait to start on again as we slowly emerge from the Pandemic.

Warren has been married to his beautiful wife Carol for 33 years, and they are the proud parents of one daughter, Suzette, and one granddaughter, Danae Mia, affectionately known as Mia – yes, the same Mia who is featured in "Mia Goes to Jamaica" and "Always Be Your Best You."

CPSIA information can be obtained
at www.ICGtesting.com
Printed in the USA
LVHW072019041121
702388LV00001B/3